Learning the Cello

Book Two

For individual study,
single-string classes, or
mixed-string classes

by Cassia Harvey

CHP287

www.charveypublications.com

1. D, E, F♯, G, and A

2. Double Note Exercise

3. Eighth Note Challenge

4. March of the Manatees

5. A La Claire Fontaine

6. The Notes on the D String

7. The Notes on the A String

8. Playing on D and A

9. Clarke's Trumpet Voluntary

10. Theme from Handel's *Music from the Royal Fireworks*

11. D Scale Exercise

6 = 6 beats in a measure
8 = an eighth note gets one beat

♪ = 1 beat   ♪. = 3 beats

12. D Scale in 6/8

13. Lullaby: A Round

14. I'd Like to Sing: A Round

15. D Major Running

16. Cucaracha Exercise

17. La Cucaracha

18. A Tricky Study

19. When the Saints Go Marching In

20. Marching Exercise

21. 'When the Saints' Variation

22. String Crossing Workout

23. Bach's March

24. Caisson Exercise

25. The Caissons are Rolling Along

26. D Major Skipping

27. Slurs:

When you get to the middle of the bow, switch to another string, but keep your bow moving in the same direction.

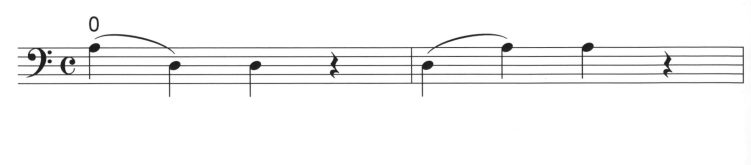

28. Cape Cod Workout

29. Cape Cod Chantey

30. Arpeggios in D

31. Slur Practice

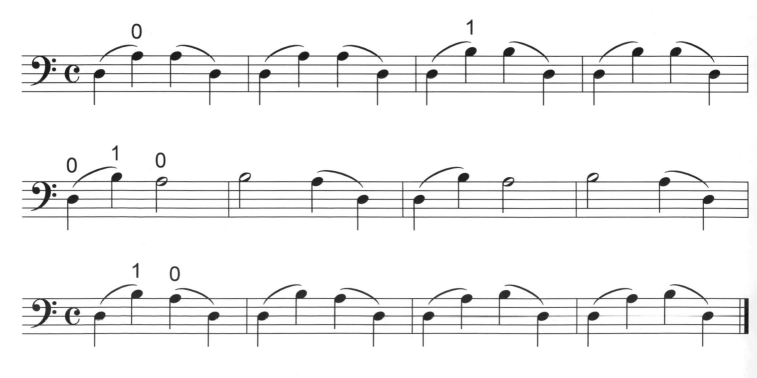

32. Bow, Belinda

33. Chatter with the Angels

34. Cow in the Pasture

Retake your bow
& start at the frog
on the next line.

35. Little Silver Moon

6 = 6 beats in a measure
8 = an eighth note gets one beat

36. 6/8 Study

37. Funiculi Funicula

38. D Scale in 6/8

39. Pop Goes the Weasel

40. 6/8 Etude

41. O'Carroll Practice

42. Paddy O'Carroll

43. Dotted Quarter Notes

If we take one eighth note away from a quarter note and give it to the first quarter note, it is written with a dot (.)

44. Jazzy Comin' Round the Mountain

45. Dandy Exercise

46. Cohan's Yankee Doodle Boy

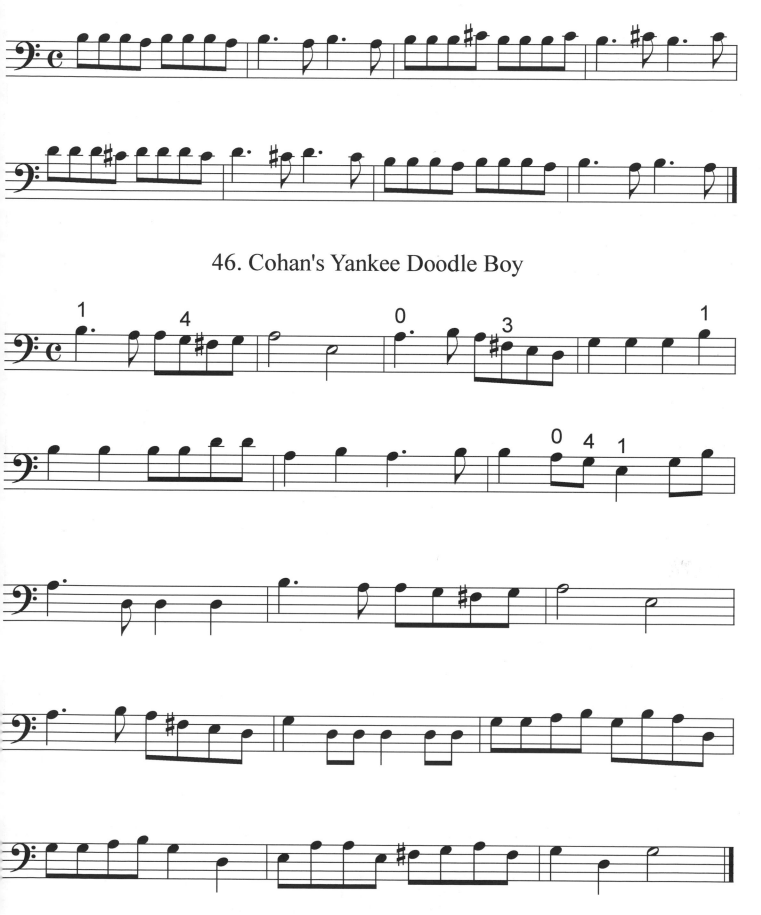

47. Slurs Between Two Fingers

48. Lullaby

49. Slurs on the Up-Bow

50. Loch Lomond

51. Slurs on a D Major Scale

52. Stephen Foster's "Nelly Bly"

53. Slurs on Intervals

54. Stephen Foster's 'Camptown Races'

55. The Notes on the G String

56. G String Reading

57. G String Challenge!

58. Feeling the Rhythm

59. Contredans

60. Epanay: A Sioux Chant

61. Little Scales on the G String

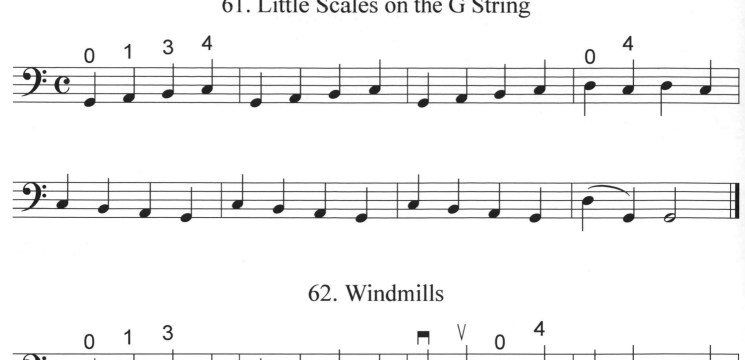

62. Windmills

63. 6/8 on the G String

Dynamics: *p* means piano (soft)   *mf* means mezzo-forte (medium loud)
           f means forte (loud)

64. Reuben and Rachel Variation

65. Fire Chant

66. Old Train's A-Coming

67. G Major Exercise

68. French-Canadian Folk Song

69. Slur Challenge

70. Go in Peace

71. Dotted Eights in 3/4

72. My Bonnie Lies Over the Ocean

73. Handel's March

74. A Traditional Lullaby

75. Finger Workout

76. Cotton-Eyed Joe (running)

77. Bowing Study

78. Cotton-Eyed Joe

79. March Warm-Up

80. Colonel Bogey's March, by Lieutenant Ricketts

81. Come Follow Me; a Round

82. Extend to Reach High 2nd Finger and 4th Finger

Extend 2nd finger to reach F♯, then play 4th finger on G♯. Slide the thumb up under 2nd finger to help the hand stretch.

83. Extension Practice

84. Extension Training

85. Lazy Summer Day

86. Country Gardens

87. Plow Exercise

88. Speed the Plow

89. Stretching Exercise

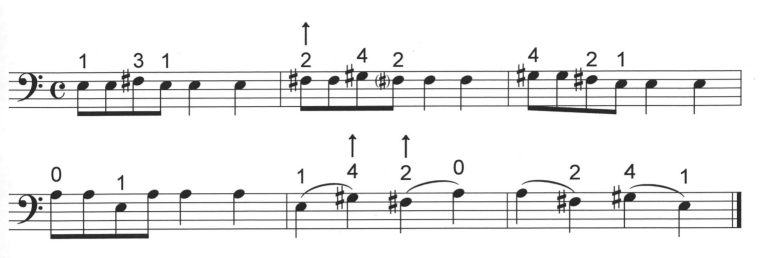

90. Yanayev's "The Winter Palace"

91. Cellos and Violas Learn the Notes on the C String

92. C String Patterns

93. Little C String Scales

94. Zum Gali

95. Jim Along Josie

96. An Awkward Exercise!

97. Jubilee

means crescendo (get louder)

means decrescendo (get softer)

98. There's a Hole in the Bucket, Dear Liza

99. Lavender's Blue

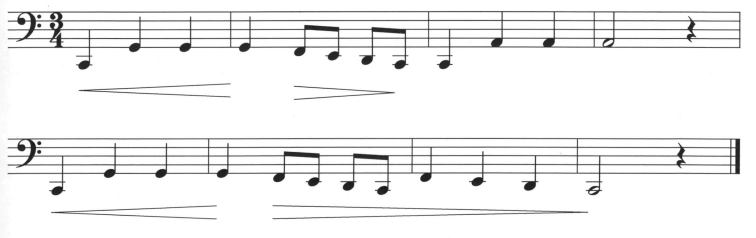

100. Down and Up Bows

101. Pickup Notes: Start on an Up Bow (V)

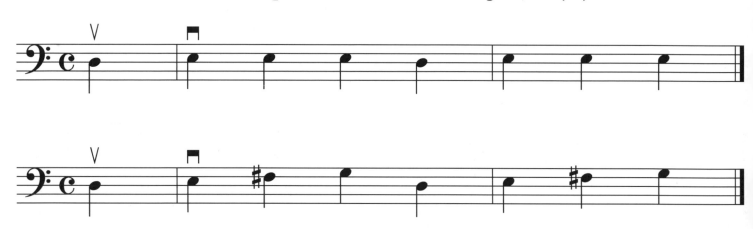

102. Hunter's Chorus Exercise #1: Pickup Notes and Double Up-Bows

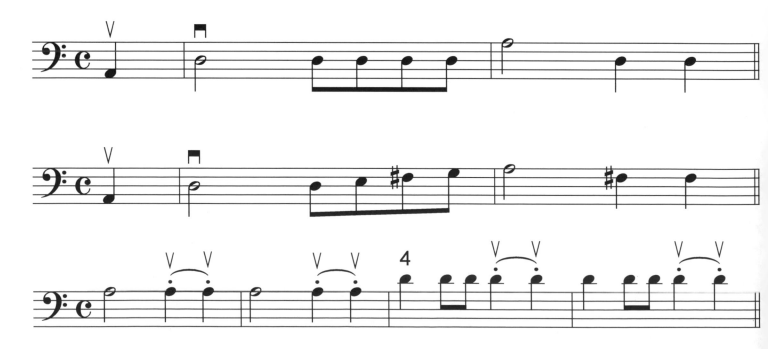

103. Hunter's Chorus Exercise #2: Finger Exercise

104. Hunter's Chorus Exercise #3: Tricky Patterns

105. Hunter's Chorus Exercise #4: String Crossing

106. Hunter's Chorus by Von Weber

107. 2nd Finger

108. Sad Frere Jacques

109. 2nd Finger on D and A

110. Soldier's Joy

111. 2nd Finger Study

112. San Sereni

113. Extending

114. 6/8 and Extending

115. Britches Full of Stitches

116. Stitching Variation No. 1

117. Stretching Practice

118. Stitching Variation No. 2

119. 2nd and 3rd Fingers

120. Arkansas Traveler

121. F♮ Study

If there are no # signs in the key signature
at the beginning of the line, or in the measure
before the note, every F will be an F♮.

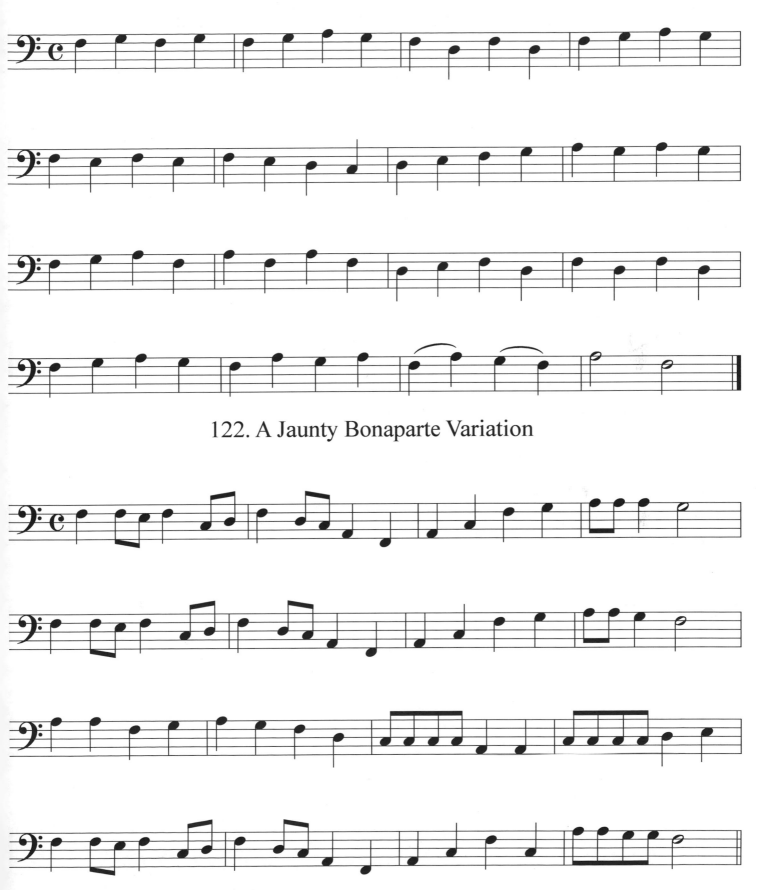

122. A Jaunty Bonaparte Variation

123. D Major Scale and Arpeggios

When there are two # signs in the key signature at the beginning of the line, every F and every C will be F♯ and C♯.

Play both strings together; this is a "double-stop."

124. Don't Fly Yet! (a fiddle tune)

125. G Major Scale, Arpeggio, and Broken Thirds

126. Crandall's Song: "Dude! Dude! Dude!"

127. G Major Exercise

128. The Irish Washerwoman (a fiddle tune)

129. C Major Scale and Arpeggios

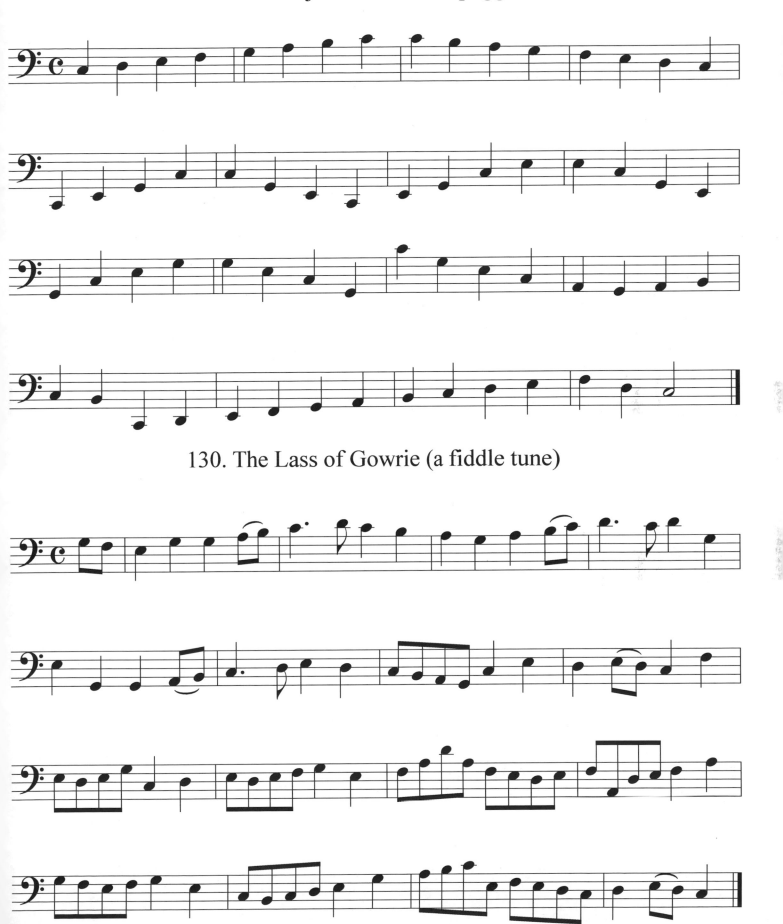

130. The Lass of Gowrie (a fiddle tune)

131. F Major Scale and Arpeggios

132. Auld Lang Syne (the New Year's Song)

Beginning Fiddle Duets for Two Cellos

Cripple Creek

Trad., arr. Myanna Harvey

78860181R00038

Made in the USA
Middletown, DE
05 July 2018